GW00319519

Kuo Huey Jen

Regional Chinese Specialities

Cookery Editor Sonia Allison
Series Editor Wendy Hobson

foulsham

Foreword

Chinese food and traditional methods of cooking go back thousands of years. The range and variety is immense, partly because of the marked regional differences over such a vast country. So a culinary journey through China is almost endless, so great is its variety of dishes.

Markets abound everywhere selling morning-fresh meat, game and poultry, shellfish, sea and river fish, fruit and often curious-looking vegetables – at least to a foreigner's eye – while myriads of herbal remedies, assorted teas and kitchen equipment are piled high for the locals to look at, haggle over and buy or not, as the mood takes them.

'Heaven loves those who eat well' is an old Chinese proverb and certainly the Chinese tuck into their food with glee and surprising speed, deftly wielding chopsticks as they tackle one course after the other, sipping perfumed tea in between bites and devouring with obvious devotion what has been described as the most cultured and classic gastronomy in the world.

Contents

Cooking with Tradition

The Chinese love their food and respect the traditions of food preparation, cooking and serving which have been handed down for generations.

Regional Cooking

Broadly speaking, there are six main culinary regions in China and while many techniques and ingredients cross the boundaries, each region has a particular and distinctive style.

Peking
Peking cooking, best known for its exclusive and costly Peking duck, is to be found in this cooler, north-eastern part of China as are spicy and well-seasoned hot pots made from lamb or beef, intermingled with onions, garlic, ginger, chives and leeks. Also famous is the famous Mongolian Fire Pot (resembling Switzerland's fondue Chinoise), unleavened breads, noodles, carp, giant prawns and crab. Shanghai cooking is much the same as Peking but, being a cosmopolitan centre and melting pot for tourists, is also an area where other regional dishes are well-represented.

Canton
Cantonese cooking is what Westerners are most familiar with both because of easier contact with and greater emigration from this region. This particular part of the country has a greater variety of dishes than anywhere else and is noted for recipes made from ultra-fresh fish, meat, poultry and vegetables, well-spiced yet light in character and easy to digest. Dim sum, or 'little heart' also belongs to this south-eastern region and comprises up to thirty or more sweet and savoury dishes plus two or three soups in immense pots, all served piping hot in or from little bamboo baskets stacked one on top of the other. You can take your pick from braised chicken feet, giblets, steamed dumplings containing meat or fish, spring rolls, deep-fried tofu, fried turnovers and other mystic fantasies such as fortune cookies – little crunchy biscuits with a prophetic message printed on a piece of paper enclosed in each one.

Szechuan
In the west of the country, in the province of Szechuan, the food is hot and spicy, as though to counteract the heat and humidity. Chillies are used in abundance, so too are salted tofu, mushrooms and noodles with accompaniments of tinglingly sharp, zesty pickles. The most popular methods of cooking here are deep-frying, steaming and smoking.

Hunan
Hunan, lying inland north-east of Szechuan, reputedly serves the best deep-fried river carp in China. It is also the home of sweet-sour dishes, uses wine in cooking, prefers noodles to rice and, being a wheat-growing area, also has a large recipe collection of superb steamed and baked breads.

Fukien

Fukien is also east, on the coast situated between Canton and Shanghai and virtually opposite Taiwan. Soups are excellent in this region. Sometimes as many as four are served at a meal, and also much enjoyed are roast suckling pig, every conceivable seafood you can think of, rice as an accompaniment and soy sauce with everything. China's finest soy sauces are produced here. This is probably where surf and turf originated (fish eaten together with meat) and the most widely used cooking methods are steaming and braising.

Mandarin

Mandarin food, once served to the fastidious and aristocratic mandarins, is a sumptuous combination of the best of Peking and Shanghai cooking.

Notes on the Recipes

1 Follow one set of measurements only, do not mix metric and Imperial.
2 Eggs are size 2.
3 Wash fresh produce before preparation.
4 Spoon measurements are level.
5 Adjust seasoning and strongly-flavoured ingredients, such as onions and garlic, to suit your own taste.
6 If you substitute dried for fresh herbs, use only half the amount specified.
7 Preparation times refer to preparation and cooking and are approximate.

Pleasures of the Chinese Table

A land such as China that can look back on a long culinary tradition, has naturally given rise to the development of an indigenous food culture quite different from that in the West. For the Chinese, eating is essential to both physical and spiritual well-being. A Chinese meal is an achievement of harmony of the colour, texture, aroma and flavour of the foods, balancing all the various elements to produce a delicious and satisfying meal.

Everyday meals do not have to be opulent – a simple combination of rice or noodles with one or two meat or fish dishes and a soup. Celebrations, on the other hand, are to be shared with family and friends and the meals must be magnificent – twenty or more courses is not unusual. Every region, even every family, has its own particular characteristics, traditions and rules to be observed. A fixed order of courses, as you find in a Western restaurant, does not exist. The important thing is the interaction and contrast of the single components of the meal.

The Chinese are masters of their art and in view of the variety of dishes they produce, Western observers are often amazed at the basic equipment to be found in

a Chinese kitchen. By comparison with European kitchens, the Chinese kitchen is extremely sparsely equipped. At its centre is the wok, often built in, the size of which will vary depending on how many people the cook normally caters for. The Chinese do not bother with lots of knives, like those so often used

by European cooks. A chopping knife in perhaps three sizes is sufficient, and anyone who has watched a Chinese cook preparing meat or vegetables will know with what artistry they weld their knives, making from the smallest vegetables the most perfect piece of art.

The preparation of any meal, but particularly of a

celebratory one, is vital so that the course of the meal is not disrupted and the dishes are served quickly one after the other. Because of the different cooking methods, a festive meal may take up to a week to prepare. Many dishes will be enhanced with dried ingredients requiring up to three days soaking, or cooking methods may be combined, so that an ingredient which is pre-boiled, might then be fried or smoked. Even stir-fried dishes which spend only a few minutes in the hot wok before serving, include ingredients which have been carefully prepared, sliced and chopped beforehand.

The preparation of the table is equally important so that the meal can be beautifully presented. The table will be covered with a white cloth and festively decorated. Dishes, glasses, plates, chopsticks and bowls of the various sauces will be attractive arranged around a large revolving plate in the centre on which each course is placed.

Everyone at the table helps themselves to the food in the centre. Once the plate is empty, it is taken away and a new dish brought in. The quantities which can be eaten may seem large, but the host always serves more than is necessary. If everything is eaten and nothing remains, this is an indication that the guests are still hungry. Only when his guests start just nibbling at the fancy delicacies offered is a good host satisfied and will call for the last course, usually a soup, the stock in which the various dishes were cooked, served with a generous bowl of rice.

Cooking Techniques

At the heart of all Chinese cooking are the techniques handed down and followed precisely to ensure that the food retains its taste, colour and consistency. Whether cooked until crisp, firm to the bite, or so soft it falls from the bone, each ingredient is cooked in the way that will bring out its best qualities.

Thickening Sauces

If a sauce has not reached the consistency you prefer while cooking, you can easily thicken it before serving. The traditional method of thickening a Chinese sauce is to mix a little cornflour to a smooth paste with a spoonful of water. Stir this into the sauce, bring to the boil and simmer gently for a few minutes, stirring well, until the sauce has thickened to your liking.

Stir-Frying

A traditional method of preparing food, stir-frying is best done in a wok which can be heated to the necessary high temperature and in which you can stir foods without them spilling over the edge of the pan. For perfect stir-frying, a little oil is heated in the wok then smallish cubes or strips of food are tossed and stirred together as they are rapidly fried in the hot oil. Those foods which take longest to cook, such as meat, go into the wok first then moved to the sides to keep warm as other foods are added and stir-fried.

Braising

A more sophisticated technique, braising is used for foods which require longer cooking. They are first briefly fried, then liquid is added in which the foods cook. The technique is often called red-braising, as the cooking liquid often contains dark soy sauce, Chinese wine or sherry, sugar, spices and grated orange rind which turns the food a deep mahogany red as it cooks.

Roasting

A popular cooking method, this is carried out in communal ovens as the average domestic kitchen is too small to house its own. For smallish pieces of food, a wok or frying pan is used instead.

Deep and Shallow Frying

When deep-frying, Chinese use very hot oil heated in the wok. Small pieces of food, usually coated in flour or batter, are plunged into the oil and fried until cooked and golden brown. The wok or a frying pan is also suitable for shallow frying when foods are cooked with just enough oil to prevent sticking.

Simmering

This is a method of very slow stewing in which meat and poultry are cooked gently, just below the boil, until they are so tender that the meat falls from the bones. Chunks of vegetables are added at the end of cooking so that they are tender but retain a slight crispness.

Steaming

For steaming, food is cooked in bamboo baskets, often one on top of the other, over gently simmering water or stock. If the food is savoury, salt is added to the water or stock; if sweet, sugar is added. It is a popular method of cooking in China and used for dumplings, bread rolls and dim sum.

Special Ingredients

Chinese cooks take particular care to use only the freshest ingredients and will also search for unusual ingredients and products at the market to surprise and delight guests.

It is easy to find most ingredients for Chinese cooking in supermarkets or fresh vegetable markets. For those ingredients which are slightly more unusual, you may need to go to a delicatessen or Oriental store.

Rice
Rice or noodles are always served with any Chinese meal. Supermarkets and Oriental shops often sell Chinese rice, which tends to be slightly more sticky than other varieties, although you can always use long-grain rice if you prefer.

Egg Noodles
Chinese egg noodles are made of wheat, eggs, water and salt. They are sold dried and are widely available.

Rice Wine
Chinese rice wine is a traditional drink used both in cooking and as a beverage. It is made from rice, yeast and water and tastes similar to dry sherry, which can be used as a substitute if necessary.

Coriander
Coriander, sometimes known as Chinese parsley, is similar to parsley but has a more distinctive flavour. It is available in supermarkets, but parsley can be used instead, if necessary.

Transparent Noodles
Also called glass, bean thread or cellophane noodles, these are thin, white noodles made from soy bean flour. They have a neutral taste and will absorb or complement stronger flavours. They should be soaked for a short time before boiling, or deep-fried without pre-soaking.

Bamboo Shoots
Fresh bamboo shoots are harvested twice a year in China, but in the West they are usually only available in cans. The large, thick parts of the plant are cut into strips, slices or cubed and cooked briefly.

Mangetout
Also called sugar peas, these are readily available fresh or frozen. They should be cooked only for a very short time to retain their delicate flavour and crisp texture.

Szechuan Peppers
Szechuan peppercorns are slightly milder than black and have a pleasantly aromatic and distinctive flavour. They are available dried and lightly roasted.

Five-Spice Powder
This is a typical Oriental combination of spices blended from fennel, star anise, cloves, cinnamon, ginger with a liquorice-like aroma. It is readily available in supermarkets.

Chilli Peppers
A strong, small and fiery member of the capsicum family, chilli peppers can be red, yellow or green. Discard the seeds for a milder flavour and wash your hands after preparing peppers as they contain an irritant which will sting your mouth or eyes if you touch them.

Root Ginger
A well-used spice in Eastern cooking, root ginger has a warm and distinctive taste. It should be peeled and grated or finely chopped before use. Ground ginger, crystallised ginger or ginger preserved in syrup are also available but should only be used where specified as they will not have the same flavour.

Lotus
Native to Asia, lotus is a vegetable belonging to the water lily family and is found growing below water level as strings of elongated swollen roots with leaves and flowers on the surface. It can be omitted from recipes if unavailable, or substituted with bamboo shoots.

Soy Beansprouts
Soy beansprouts have been used in Chinese cooking for centuries. They are available both fresh and canned from most supermarkets.

Dried Chinese Mushrooms
These are available in large supermarkets, delicatessens or Oriental food shops. They need to be soaked in hot water for at least 30 minutes before using, according to the recipe instructions. The tough stems are discarded after soaking.

Wood Ear Mushrooms
Another variety of dried mushrooms, these large mushrooms should be chopped before soaking. The hard stems are discarded.

Lily Buds
An important ingredient in Chinese cooking, lily buds are available dried from Oriental shops. They are light brown in colour and need soaking in hot water for at least 30 minutes before use. Their aroma is distinctively woody.

Soy Sauce
Soy sauce is a dilution of soy beans, cereals (mostly rice) and spices. It is available as dark, medium and light, the most frequently used.

Plum Sauce
This is a piquant, sweet-tasting condiment used to accompany Peking duck. It is made of puréed plums and apricots seasoned with five-spice powder, chilli, vinegar, garlic and sugar.

Hoisin Sauce
A seasoning sauce made from soy sauce, soy bean paste and soy beans as well as garlic, vinegar and sugar, hoisin sauce adds a piquant, sweet-sour flavour to many dishes.

Oyster Sauce
A condiment made from soy sauce, rice wine and stock simmered with oysters and mussels and sometimes crabs and sugar, this is readily available in supermarkets.

Chilli Sauce
Many varieties of chilli sauce are available which can enliven simple dishes.

Tofu
Tofu is soy bean curd compressed into a creamy-white cake which looks a little like soft cheese. It is used in many Chinese recipes and has a very bland flavour which readily absorbs the stronger flavours of accompanying ingredients.

Vegetable Dishes

Vegetables form an important part of Chinese cooking and figure heavily in many recipes. Quick-cooking techniques are particularly suited to creating flavoursome dishes.

Ten Vegetables, page 18

17

Ten Vegetables

Serves 4
Preparation time: 30 mins
plus soaking time
225 kcal

---

*6-8 dried wood ear
mushrooms*

*20 ml/4 tsp lily buds
(optional)*

*100 g/4 oz transparent
noodles*

1 bunch spring onions

1 red pepper

*100 g/4 oz bamboo shoots,
canned, drained*

75 ml/5 tbsp groundnut oil

100 g/4 oz mangetout

100 g/4 oz bean sprouts

*150 ml/¹/₄ pt/²/₃ cup
vegetable stock*

30 ml/2 tbsp soy sauce

15 ml/1 tbsp hoisin sauce

*5 ml/1 tsp rice wine or
sherry*

5 ml/1 tsp vinegar

5 ml/1 tsp five-spice powder

2 slices pineapple, diced

*2 ginger knobs, preserved
in syrup, sliced*

*salt and freshly ground
Szechuan pepper*

---

1 In 3 separate bowls,
soak the mushrooms, lily
buds and transparent
noodles in hot water for 45
minutes.
2 Meanwhile, trim the
spring onions and cut into
strips. Halve and deseed
the pepper and also cut
into strips. Cut the bam-
boo shoots into strips.

3 Drain the mushrooms
and the lily buds. Cut the
mushrooms into small
pieces, discarding the
hard stems. Thoroughly
drain the noodles.
4 Heat up the oil, add the
mushrooms and lily buds
and fry briskly for about 2
minutes.
5 Add all the vegetables
and stir-fry for 2 to 3
minutes.
6 Stir in the stock. Mix in
the soy sauce, hoisin
sauce, rice wine, wine vinegar and five-spice
powder.
7 Mix in the pineapple,
ginger and noodles. Heat
thoroughly stirring. Sea-
son with salt and
szechuan pepper.

Photograph page 16

Fried Vegetables with Prawns

Serves 4
Preparation time: 30 mins
plus marinating time
395 kcal

---

*4-6 dried Chinese
mushrooms*

400 g/14 oz peeled prawns

30 ml/2 tbsp soy sauce

30 ml/2 tbsp oyster sauce

45 ml/3 tbsp rice wine

juice of 1 lemon

4 spring onions

100 g/4 oz mangetout

*100 g/4 oz canned bamboo
shoots, drained*

1 red pepper

1 green pepper

100 g/4 oz bean sprouts

30 ml/2 tbsp groundnut oil

*400 g/4 oz cooked noodles
(125 g/5 oz uncooked)*

*150 ml/¹/₄ pt/²/₃ cup
vegetable stock*

*salt and freshly ground
pepper*

a pinch of cayenne pepper

---

1 Soak the mushrooms in
hot water for 30 minutes.
Marinate the prawns in the
soy sauce, oyster sauce,
rice wine and lemon juice
for 10 to 15 minutes.
2 Drain the mushrooms
then cut into strips.
3 Slice the vegetables
into small strips.
4 Heat the oil, add the
vegetables and fry, stir-
ring all the time, for 3
minutes.
5 Add the prawns with the
marinade, the noodles
and the stock, bring to the
boil and season to taste
with salt and cayenne
pepper. Simmer for 2 min-
utes then serve
immediately.

Photograph opposite

Red-Braised China Cabbage

Serves 4
Preparation time: 30 mins
plus soaking time
220 kcal

6-8 dried Chinese mushrooms
1 dried chilli pepper
450 g/1 *lb* Chinese cabbage
4 spring onions
45 ml/*3 tbsp* groundnut oil
45 ml/*3 tbsp* soy sauce
10 ml/*2 tsp* hoisin sauce
45 ml/*3 tbsp* rice wine
150 ml/*¹/₄ pt/²/₃* cup vegetable stock
5 ml/*1 tsp* sugar
salt and freshly ground black pepper
¹/₂ bunch parsley, chopped

1 Soak the mushrooms and chilli pepper in hot water for 45 minutes.
2 Cut the Chinese cabbage into 3 cm squares. Cut the spring onions and cut into 2 cm/1 in pieces.
3 Heat the oil, add the vegetables and fry briskly for about 3 to 4 minutes, turning all the time.
4 Chop the mushrooms and chilli peppers. Add them to the pan and fry for a further 5 minutes.
5 Add the soy and hoisin sauces, the rice wine and stock and bring to the boil. Braise the vegetables for 4 to 5 minutes, season with salt and pepper and sprinkle with the chopped parsley.

Photograph (top)

Red-Cooked Sprouts

Serves 4
Preparation time: 30 mins
360 kcal

6-8 dried Chinese mushrooms
400 g/14 oz canned bamboo shoots
30 ml/2 tbsp groundnut oil
200 g/7 oz minced pork
4 spring onions, diced
1 red pepper, diced
100 g/3 oz soy beansprouts
150 ml/¹/₄ pt/²/₃ cup stock
45 ml/3 tbsp rice wine
30 ml/2 tbsp soy sauce
30 ml/2 tbsp hoisin sauce
10 ml/2 tsp chilli sauce
salt and freshly ground black pepper
a pinch of sugar
10 ml/2 tsp cornflour
20 ml/4 tsp water

1 Soak the mushrooms in hot water for 45 minutes.
2 Drain and cut them and the bamboo shoots into strips.
3 Heat the oil and fry the pork briskly. Add the spring onions and pepper and fry for 4 minutes.
4 Add the beansprouts, bamboo shoots and mushrooms.
5 Add the stock, rice wine, soy, hoisin and chilli sauces and bring to the boil. Season.
6 Mix the cornflour and water, stir into the sauce and simmer until thickened.

Photograph (bottom)

Vegetables with Tofu

Serves 4
Preparation time: 30 mins
320 kcal

---

4 spring onions

1 red pepper

30 ml/*2 tbsp* groundnut oil

6-8 dried Chinese mushrooms

400 g/*14 oz* tofu, cubed

salt and freshly ground black pepper

100 g/*4 oz* beansprouts

30 ml/*2 tbsp* soy sauce

45 ml/*3 tbsp* rice wine or sherry

5 ml/*1 tsp* grated ginger root

5 ml/*1 tsp* sugar

150 ml/*1/4 pt/2/3* cup vegetable stock

10 ml/*2 tsp* cornflour

20 ml/*4 tsp* water

1/2 bunch chives, chopped

---

1 Soak the mushrooms in hot water for 45 minutes, then drain and slice.
2 Clean the spring onions, cut them into 2 cm/1 in pieces. Cut the pepper into strips.
3 Heat half the oil in a frying pan, add the tofu and fry for about 3 minutes, stirring all the time. Season with salt and pepper. Remove the tofu and place on a dish, pour over the soy sauce and rice wine or sherry and season with ginger and sugar.
4 Heat the remaining oil and stir-fry the vegetables for 3 minutes. Add the stock and bring to the boil.
5 Mix together the cornflour and water, stir in and simmer until thickened. Return all the ingredients to the pan to heat through before serving.

Photograph opposite (top)

Three-Vegetable Stir-Fry

Serves 4
Preparation time: 30 mins
300 kcal

---

225 g/*8 oz* white cabbage

225 g/*8 oz* Chinese cabbage

225 g/*8 oz* leeks

45 ml/*3 tbsp* sesame oil

30 ml/*2 tbsp* soy sauce

30 ml/*2 tbsp* fruit vinegar

15 ml/*1 tbsp* sugar

15 ml/*1 tbsp* plum sauce

salt and freshly ground white pepper

1 bunch chives, chopped

---

1 Cut cabbage and Chinese leaves into 1 cm/1/2 inch strips.
2 Halve the leeks lengthwise, wash under running water and cut into strips.
3 Heat the sesame oil, add the vegetables and stir-fry for about 5 to 6 minutes.
4 Stir in the soy sauce, fruit vinegar, sugar and plum sauce and season with salt and pepper.
5 Serve sprinkled with freshly cut chives.

Photograph opposite (bottom)

Sweet-Sour
Savoy Cabbage
with Ham

Serves 4
Preparation time: 30 mins
350 kcal

4-6 wood ear mushrooms

1 small savoy cabbage

45 ml/3 tbsp groundnut oil

1 onion, chopped

1 clove garlic, chopped

300 ml/¹/₂ pt/1¹/₄ cups stock

30 ml/2 tbsp soy sauce

15 ml/1 tbsp tomato purée

30 ml/2 tbsp fruit vinegar

15 ml/1 tbsp honey

salt and freshly ground black pepper

5 ml/1 tsp five-spice powder

100 g/4 oz uncooked ham, chopped

10 ml/2 tsp cornflour

20 ml/4 tsp water

a few drops of tabasco sauce

---

1 Soak the mushrooms in hot water for 45 minutes. Drain and cut into strips.
2 Cut the savoy cabbage into strips.
3 Heat the oil, add the vegetables and stir-fry for about 5 minutes.
4 Add the stock, seasonings and ham then bring to the boil.
5 Blend the cornflour with the water and stir in. Add the tabasco sauce. Bring to the boil and simmer for 2 minutes.

Photograph (left)

Swede with Chicken and Ham

Serves 4
Preparation time: 35 mins
340 kcal

600 g/1¼ lb swede
2 chicken breast fillets
75 g/3 oz gammon
2 onions
2 cloves garlic
salt
30 ml/2 tbsp sesame oil
5 ml/2 tsp grated ginger root
45 ml/3 tbsp soy sauce
45 ml/3 tbsp rice wine or sherry
150 ml/¼ pt/⅔ cup vegetable stock
freshly ground black pepper
a pinch of coriander
a pinch of nutmeg
a pinch of cloves
a pinch of sugar

1 Cut the swede and onions into bite-sized pieces. Cut the chicken and gammon into strips
2 Crush the garlic with salt until it forms a paste.
3 Heat the oil, add the swede, chicken, gammon, onions, garlic and stir-fry for 3 minutes.
4 Pour on the soy sauce, rice wine or sherry and stock. Bring to the boil then cover and simmer for about 15 to 20 minutes until the swede is tender.
5 Season to taste with the spices.

Photograph (right)

Braised Vegetables

Serves 4
Preparation time: 30 mins
plus soaking time
260 kcal

4-6 dried Chinese mushrooms

6-8 wood ear mushrooms

100 g/4 oz tofu

2 carrots

1 small leek

3 celery sticks

50 g/2 oz rettich (white radish)

45 ml/3 tbsp groundnut oil

100 g/4 oz bamboo shoots, drained

1 onion, chopped

1 clove garlic, chopped

100 g/4 oz lotus roots or bamboo shoots, drained

100 g/4 oz soy beansprouts

250 ml/8 fl oz/1 cup vegetable stock

30 ml/2 tbsp soy sauce

30 ml/2 tbsp plum sauce

30 ml/2 tbsp wine vinegar

salt and freshly ground black pepper

a pinch of cayenne pepper

a pinch of sugar

1 bunch chives, chopped

1 Soak the mushrooms in hot water for 45 minutes. Cut the tofu into strips.
2 Cut the carrots, leek, celery, rettich and bamboo shoots into strips. Cut the lotus roots into bite-size pieces.
3 Heat the oil in a frying pan, add the onion and garlic and fry until pale gold. Add the carrots, leek, celery and the rettich and stir-fry for 4 to 5 minutes. Drain and slice the mushrooms and add with tofu.
4 Add the lotus roots, soy beansprouts and bamboo shoots and stir-fry for another 4 to 5 minutes.
5 Add the stock, soy and plum sauces and wine vinegar and bring to the boil, stirring.
6 Season the vegetables well with the spices and serve sprinkled with chives.

Photograph opposite (top)

Gourmet Tip
The Chinese like to eat braised vegetables served on a bed of noodles or egg noodles.

Pearl Vegetables with Chicken Cream

Serves 4
Preparation time: 50 mins
290 kcal

---

350 g/12 oz carrots, cubed

1 small rettich, cubed

1 courgette, cubed

salt

30 ml/2 tbsp groundnut oil

2 chicken breast fillets, finely minced

3 egg whites

15 ml/1 tbsp cornflour

300 ml/¹/₂ pt/1¹/₄ cups vegetable stock

freshly ground black pepper

a pinch of nutmeg

a pinch of ground cloves

a pinch of cayenne pepper

a pinch of ground ginger

1 bunch chives, chopped

1 small honeydew melon, the flesh spooned into balls

1 Blanch the vegetables in boiling salted water for 3 minutes then drain.
2 Heat the oil, add the vegetables and stir-fry for about 6 minutes. Remove to a dish.
3 Mix the meat with the egg whites, cornflour and stock.
4 Season well with salt and pepper, put into the frying pan and cook until it turns into a creamy, light-coloured mixture, stirring continuously. Stir in the seasonings and spices.
5 Arrange the vegetables in a dish, coat with the meat mixture and sprinkle with freshly chopped chives. Garnish with melon balls.

Photograph opposite (bottom)

Mangetout with Mushrooms

Serves 4
Preparation time: 30 mins
260 kcal

6-8 dried Chinese mushrooms

4-6 wood ear mushrooms

30 ml/**2 tbsp** groundnut oil

4 spring onions, sliced

450 g/**1 lb** mangetout

1 clove garlic, finely chopped

150 ml/**¼ pt/²⁄₃ cup** vegetable stock

15 ml/**1 tbsp** soy sauce

15 ml/**1 tbsp** fruit vinegar

15 ml/**1 tbsp** honey

salt and freshly ground black pepper

a pinch of Cayenne pepper

½ bunch fresh coriander, chopped

---

1 Soak the mushrooms in hot water for 45 minutes. Drain and cut into strips.
2 Heat the oil, add the vegetables and the mushrooms and stir-fry for about 3 to 4 minutes.
3 Mix together the stock, soy sauce, fruit vinegar and honey. Add to the vegetables and bring the mixture to the boil. Simmer for 2 minutes, stirring.
4 Season well with salt and pepper and sprinkle with finely chopped coriander. Serve immediately.

Photograph opposite (top)

Quick Soy Bean Vegetables

Serves 4
Preparation time: 20 mins
250 kcal

---

1 bunch spring onions

2 garlic cloves

salt

45 ml/**3 tbsp** sesame oil

1 knob of ginger, preserved in syrup, diced

450 g/**1 lb** soy beansprouts

45 ml/**3 tbsp** vegetable stock

30 ml/**2 tbsp** soy sauce

15 ml/**1 tbsp** hoisin sauce

salt and freshly ground white pepper

a pinch of Cayenne pepper

a pinch of sugar

½ bunch chives, chopped

---

1 Cut the spring onions and cut into shortish pieces. Peel the garlic cloves and crush with the salt.
2 Heat the sesame oil, add the vegetables and stir-fry for 3 to 4 minutes.
3 Stir in the stock, soy sauce and hoisin sauce then bring to the boil. Simmer for 2 minutes, stirring.
4 Season the vegetables well with salt, pepper, Cayenne pepper and sugar and serve sprinkled with chives.

Photograph opposite (centre)

Cabbage Stir-Fry

Serves 4
Preparation time: 30 mins
185 kcal

---

750 g/**1 1/4 lb** white cabbage

1 red pepper

salt

30 ml/**2 tbsp** groundnut oil

1 small chilli pepper, chopped

1 clove garlic, chopped

1 onion, chopped

10 ml/**2 tsp** grated ginger root

15 ml/**1 tbsp** tomato purée

30 ml/**2 tbsp** wine vinegar

30 ml/**2 tbsp** soy sauce

5 ml/**1 tsp** sugar

freshly ground black pepper

300 ml/**½ pt/1 ¼ cups** vegetable stock

1 bunch chives, chopped

---

1 Cut the cabbage and pepper into thin strips.
2 Blanch the cabbage and pepper strips briefly in boiling salted water. Drain.
3 Heat the oil in a pan, add the vegetables and stir-fry for 5 to 6 minutes.
4 Add the ginger, tomato purée, wine vinegar, soy sauce, sugar, salt and pepper and stock. Bring to the boil and simmer for 3 to 4 minutes, stirring. Sprinkle with chives before serving.

Photograph opposite (bottom)

Meat Dishes

Chinese meat dishes not only taste delicious but as they are prepared using only the best quality, leanest meats, they offer healthy meals, too.

Sweet and Sour Pork, page 32

Sweet and Sour Pork

Serves 4
Preparation time: 35 mins
470 kcal

450 g/1 lb pork fillet
salt and freshly ground Szechuan pepper
1 egg
20 ml/4 tsp cornflour
30 ml/2 tbsp water
30 ml/2 tbsp sesame oil
1 onion
1 red pepper
2 carrots
300 ml/1/2 pt/1 1/4 cups vegetable stock
15 ml/1 tbsp tomato purée
30 ml/2 tbsp soy sauce
2 slices pineapple, diced
30 ml/2 tbsp fruit vinegar
5 ml/1 tsp curry powder
a few drops Tabasco sauce
1/2 bunch chives, chopped

1 Cut the pork fillet into very thin slices. Season well with salt and Szechuan pepper.
2 Beat the egg, cornflour and water until smooth. Add pork strips and coat each piece with egg mixture.
3 Heat the sesame oil, add the pork and stir-fry briskly for 5 minutes. Remove and leave on one side.
4 Cut the onion, pepper and carrots into strips. Add to the remaining oil in pan and stir-fry for 5 minutes.
5 Add the stock, tomato purée and soy sauce and bring to the boil.
6 Add the pineapple, fruit vinegar and curry powder. Bring back to the boil then simmer gently for 2 minutes.
7 Season with salt and pepper then add a few drops of Tabasco sauce.
8 Add the meat to the vegetables and heat through without boiling. Sprinkle with chives and serve with a crisp salad.

Photograph page 30

Gourmet Tip
Chicken, turkey or veal may be used instead of pork for this recipe.

Beef with Onions

Serves 4
Preparation time: 35 mins
390 kcal

600 g/1 1/4 lb beef fillet
salt and freshly ground black pepper
30 ml/2 tbsp soy sauce
15 ml/1 tbsp hoisin sauce
15 ml/1 tbsp rice wine or sherry
15 ml/1 tbsp honey
30 ml/2 tbsp groundnut oil
4 onions, sliced
2 carrots, cut into strips
150 ml/1/4 pt/2/3 cup vegetable stock
20 ml/5 tsp water
10 ml/2 tsp cornflour
a pinch of Cayenne pepper

1 Cut the meat into strips and season with salt and pepper.
2 Mix the soy sauce with the hoisin sauce, rice wine or sherry and honey. Pour over the meat.
3 Heat the oil in a pan or wok and briskly stir-fry the beef until cooked to taste. Remove to plate.
4 Add the vegetables to the remaining frying oil and stir-fry for 6 to 7 minutes.
5 Blend the cornflour smoothly with water, add to pan with the stock and bring just up to the boil. Return the meat to the pan and reheat. Adjust the seasoning to taste.

Photograph opposite

33

Chicken Strips with Paprika

Serves 4
Preparation time: 35 mins
440 kcal

4 chicken breast fillets
salt and freshly ground black pepper
30 ml/2 tbsp tomato ketchup
15 ml/1 tbsp honey
15 ml/1 tbsp wine vinegar
30 ml/2 tbsp soy sauce
15 ml/1 tbsp hoisin sauce
5 ml/1 tsp five-spice powder
2 onions
2 red peppers
2 green peppers
2 carrots
30 ml/2 tbsp groundnut oil
300 ml/¹/₂ pt/1 ¹/₄ cups vegetable stock
15 ml/1 tbsp cornflour
60 ml/4 tbsp water

1 Cut the chicken into strips and season with salt and pepper.
2 Mix the ketchup with the honey, vinegar, soy and hoisin sauces and five-spice powder. Stir into the meat.
3 Cut the vegetables into strips.
4 Heat the oil, add the meat and stir-fry for 5 minutes. Remove to plate. Add the vegetables and stir-fry for 5 minutes. Add the stock and return chicken to the pan.
5 Mix the cornflour with the water, stir into the pan and bring briefly to the boil.

Photograph (bottom)

Fried Chicken with Vegetables

Serves 4
Preparation time: 30 mins
415 kcal

6-8 wood ear mushrooms
4 chicken breast fillets, cubed
salt and freshly ground black pepper
30 ml/2 tbsp soy sauce
5 ml/1 tsp five-spice powder
15 ml/1 tbsp rice wine
2 eggs, beaten
20 ml/4 tsp cornflour
45 ml/3 tbsp groundnut oil
1 chilli pepper, sliced
1 onion, cut into strips
1 leek, cut into strips
2 carrots, cut into strips
100 g/4 oz celery, sliced
6 tomatoes, skinned and diced

1 Soak the mushrooms in hot water for 45 minutes. Drain and cut into strips.
2 Season the chicken with salt and pepper and place in a bowl. Mix the soy sauce, five-spice powder and rice wine and rub over the chicken.
3 Toss the chicken in the eggs. Sprinkle with cornflour.
4 Heat a little oil and fry the chicken until cooked and golden. Remove.
5 Heat the remaining oil and stir-fry the chilli pepper, onion, leek, carrots and celery for 5 minutes.
6 Add the tomatoes, mushrooms and chicken and heat through.

Photograph (top)

35

Fried Pork Nuggets

Serves 4
Preparation time: 30 mins
650 kcal

---

600 g/1 1/4 lb minced pork

2 onions, chopped

2 eggs, beaten

30 ml/2 tbsp cornflour

15 ml/1 tbsp soy sauce

15 ml/1 tbsp hoisin sauce

2 cloves garlic, crushed

5 ml/1 tsp five-spice powder

5 ml/1 tsp grated ginger root

salt and freshly ground black pepper

a pinch of Cayenne pepper

a pinch of sugar

45 ml/3 tbsp groundnut oil

1 Mix together the minced pork, onions, eggs, cornflour, soy sauce, hoisin sauce, garlic, five-spice powder and ginger.
2 Season well with salt, pepper, Cayenne pepper and sugar.
3 With damp hands, shape the meat mixture into little balls.
4 Heat the oil until sizzling, add the pork and fry until the balls are golden all over and cooked through. Turn frequently.

Photograph opposite (top)

Red-Braised Pork

Serves 4
Preparation: 2 hours
1640 kcal

1.5 kg/3 lb leg of pork

10 ml/2 tsp salt

10 ml/2 tsp sugar

5 ml/1 tsp five-spice powder

45 ml/3 tbsp soy sauce

45 ml/3 tbsp rice wine

5 ml/1 tsp freshly ground black pepper

30 ml/2 tbsp groundnut oil

1 bunch spring onions, chopped

4 carrots, diced

4 celery sticks, thinly sliced

250 ml/8 fl oz/1 cup stock

1 Score the pork skin and place in a roasting tin.
2 Mix together the salt, sugar, five-spice powder, soy sauce, rice wine and pepper. Rub into the meat then spoon over half the oil. Roast in a preheated oven at 180°C/350°F/gas mark 4 for 2 hours.
3 About 30 minutes before the end of cooking, heat the remaining oil in a wok and stir-fry the spring onions, carrots and celery until golden brown.
4 Add the stock, bring to the boil, cover and simmer gently for 25 minutes.
5 Increase the heat, remove the lid and boil until reduced by about half.
6 Carve the meat into thin slices then spoon over the vegetables and sauce.

Photograph opposite (bottom left)

Braised Lamb

Serves 4
Preparation time: 2 1/4 hours
780 kcal

1.2 kg/2 1/2 lb leg of lamb, boned

salt

4 cloves garlic, chopped

25 g/1 oz ginger root, chopped

1 chilli pepper, chopped

30 ml/2 tbsp rice wine or sherry

30 ml/2 tbsp soy sauce

300 ml/1/2 pt/1 1/4 cups vegetable stock

2 onions, sliced

2 carrots, sliced

300 g/11 oz celery, sliced

freshly ground black pepper

20 ml/4 tsp wine vinegar

2 pieces ginger preserved in syrup, chopped

1 Cut the lamb into 1 cm/1/2 in thick slices and blanch in boiling salted water until sealed.
2 Mix the garlic, ginger, chilli, pepper, rice wine, soy sauce, stock and a little salt. Pour into a pan and add the lamb. Bring to the boil then lower the heat, cover and simmer for about 1 1/2 hours or until tender.
3 About 20 minutes before the end of the cooking time, add the onions, carrots and celery. Season with pepper and vinegar and mix in the ginger.

Photograph opposite (bottom right)

Crispy Fried Duck with Fruit

Serves 4
Preparation time: 1½ hours
935 kcal

---

600 g/1¼ lb duck fillet, boned

---

2 vegetable stew packs

---

salt

---

150 ml/¼ pt/²/₃ cup rice wine or sherry

---

30 ml/2 tbsp soy sauce

---

5 ml/1 tsp five-spice powder

---

15 ml/1 tbsp hoisin sauce

---

freshly ground black pepper

---

200 g/7 oz/1¾ cups plain flour

---

150 ml/¼ pt/²/₃ cup dry white wine

---

1 egg, separated

---

oil for deep-frying

For the sauce:

---

15 ml/1 tbsp sesame oil

---

1 bunch spring onions, chopped

---

1 red pepper, diced

---

1 green pepper, diced

---

100 g/4 oz lychees, peeled and stoned

---

100 g/4 oz canned pineapple cubes

---

300 ml/½ pt/1¼ cups chicken stock

---

30 ml/2 tbsp tomato purée

---

a few drops of Tabasco sauce

---

a few drops of wine vinegar

---

15 ml/1 tbsp cornflour

---

30 ml/2 tbsp water

---

1 Cut the duck into cubes.

2 Put the vegetables into a pan of salted water and bring to the boil. Add the duck, cover and simmer for about 45 minutes. Remove duck from the pan.

3 Mix together the rice wine or sherry, soy sauce, five-spice powder, hoisin sauce and pepper. Pour over the duck and leave to marinate for 45 minutes.

4 To make the batter, beat the flour with the wine and the egg yolk until smooth. Beat the egg white until stiff and carefully fold in. Turn the duck cubes in the batter.

5 Heat the oil and deep-fry the duck until cooked. Drain well.

6 To make the sauce, heat the sesame oil in a saucepan and stir-fry the vegetables for 5 minutes. Add the lychees and pineapple and fry for 5 minutes.

7 Mix the stock and tomato purée with the remaining duck marinade, add to the vegetables and brig to the boil.

8 Season with tabasco sauce and wine vinegar according to taste. Blend the cornflour smoothly with the water, stir into the sauce and bring to the boil.

9 Return the duck to the pan and simmer for 2 minutes, until heated through, stirring continuously.

White-Cooked Duck with Vegetables

Serves 4
Preparation time: 3 hours
1195 kcal

1 oven-ready duck weighing
1½ to 2 kg/3 to 4 lb

salt

300 ml/½ pt/1¼ cups rice wine

150 ml/¼ pt/⅔ cup wine vinegar

1.5 l/2½ pts/6¼ cups vegetable stock

150 ml/¼ pt/⅔ cup soy sauce

30 ml/2 tbsp hoisin sauce

10 ml/2 tsp grated root ginger

2 chilli peppers, finely chopped

10 ml/2 tsp sugar

1 bunch spring onions, chopped

450 g/1 lb white cabbage, coarsely chopped

450 g/1 lb Chinese cabbage, coarsely chopped

salt and freshly ground black pepper

a pinch of ground coriander

a pinch of ground aniseed

5 ml/1 tsp five-spice powder

1 bunch coriander, chopped

1 Wash the duck under running water, drain well and boil for 5 minutes in salted water. Remove, rinse once more under running water and drain again.

2 Mix the rice wine, wine vinegar, stock, soy sauce and hoisin sauce and bring to the boil in a saucepan.
3 Add the ginger, chilli peppers, 10 ml/2 tsp salt and the sugar and return to the boil.
4 Add the duck to the liquid, cover and simmer for 2 to 2½ hours over a fairly gentle heat.
5 About 30 minutes before the end of cooking time, add the spring onions and white cabbage to the duck.
6 Ten minutes later, add the Chinese cabbage.
7 Season well with salt, pepper, ground coriander, aniseed and five-spice powder.
8 Continue to simmer the duck gently until the vegetables are cooked.
9 Remove the duck from the stock and slice. Sprinkle evenly with vegetables and finally garnish with the coriander.

Photograph opposite (top)

Turkey with Ginger Sauce

Serves 4
Preparation time: 30 mins
405 kcal

6-8 wood ear mushrooms

450 g/1 lb turkey breast

50 g/2 oz/½ cup cornflour

5 ml/1 tsp five-spice powder

5 ml/1 tsp freshly ground black pepper

30 ml/2 tbsp groundnut oil

2-3 chilli peppers, chopped

2-3 cloves garlic, chopped

1 bunch spring onions, chopped

10 ml/2 tsp grated root ginger

150 ml/¼ pt/⅔ cup rice wine

250 ml/8 fl oz/1 cup chicken stock

30 ml/2 tbsp soy sauce

10 ml/2 tsp cornflour

20 ml/4 tsp water

1 Soak the mushrooms in hot water for 45 minutes. Drain and cut into strips.
2 Cut the turkey into bite-size pieces.
3 Mix the cornflour with the five-spice powder and the pepper. Add the meat and coat well all over.
4 Heat the oil and stir-fry the turkey briskly until cooked. Remove from the pan.
5 Add the chill peppers and garlic to the pan and stir well. Add the spring onions and ginger and stir fry for 5 to 6 minutes.
6 Add the rice wine, stock and soy sauce and bring to the boil. Simmer for 5 minutes. Return the turkey to the pan.
7 Mix the cornflour smoothly with the water, stir into the pan and simmer until thickened.

Photograph opposite (bottom)

Fish Dishes

Chinese cooks love serving fish, and some specialise in fish dishes to the exclusion of everything else. When you try some of these recipes you may begin to understand why.

Spicy Fried Fish, page 44

Spicy Fried Fish

Serves 4
Preparation time: 45 mins
plus marinating
580 kcal

800 g/1³/₄ lb fish fillets

45 ml/**3 tbsp** soy sauce

45 ml/**3 tbsp** rice wine

salt

5 ml/**1 tsp** freshly ground black pepper

5 ml/**1 tsp** grated ginger root

1 clove garlic, chopped

300 ml/¹/₂ pt/1¹/₄ cups vegetable stock

10 ml/**2 tsp** oyster sauce

15 ml/**1 tbsp** honey

30 ml/**2 tbsp** wine vinegar

2.5 ml/¹/₂ **tsp** five-spice powder

150 ml/¹/₄ pt/²/₃ cup groundnut oil

freshly ground black pepper

a little lemon juice

¹/₂ bunch chives, chopped

1 Cut the fish fillet into strips and place in a bowl.
2 Mix the soy sauce, rice wine, salt, pepper, ginger and garlic. Pour over the fish, cover and leave to marinate in the refrigerator for at least 3 to 4 hours.
3 Remove the fish from the marinade and leave to drain well.
4 Bring the marinade to the boil with stock, oyster sauce, honey, wine vinegar and five-spice powder.

5 Place the fish in the stock and cook for about 8 minutes until just tender. Remove and drain well.
6 Heat the oil in a frying pan and carefully stir-fry the strips of fish for about 3 minutes until cooked through and golden.
7 Remove the fish, arrange on a platter and sprinkle with salt, pepper, lemon juice and chives.

Photograph page 42

Gourmet Tip
This is a recipe well-loved in China and one that uses firm fish such as sole or halibut. Avoid any fish that flakes easily.

Sweet and Sour Salmon

Serves 4
Preparation time: 45 mins
575 kcal

750 g/1¹/₂ lb salmon fillet, skinned

juice of 1 lemon

45 ml/**3 tbsp** soy sauce

45 ml/**3 tbsp** wine vinegar

salt and freshly ground white pepper

5 ml/**1 tsp** five-spice powder

5 ml/**1 tsp** sugar

2 eggs, beaten

50 g/2 oz/¹/₂ cup cornflour

oil for frying

10 ml/**2 tsp** groundnut oil

4 carrots, chopped

100 g/**4 oz** peas

1 onion, chopped

250 ml/**8 fl oz**/1 cup tomato juice

1 Cut the fish fillet into cubes, sprinkle with lemon juice, soy sauce and wine vinegar and leave to marinate for 30 minutes. Season to taste with salt, pepper, five-spice powder and sugar.
2 Remove from the marinade and coat the fish in egg, then in cornflour. Heat the oil and fry the fish until cooked. Remove from the pan and keep warm. Pour the oil out of the pan.
3 Heat the groundnut oil and stir-fry the carrots, peas and onions for 3 minutes.
4 Add the marinade and tomato juice and bring to the boil. Add the fish and reheat briefly before serving.

Photograph opposite

Carp in Sour Sauce

Serves 4
Preparation time: 35 mins
605 kcal

750 g/1 ¹/₂ lb carp fillet	
juice of 1 lemon	
45 ml/3 tbsp soy sauce	
5 ml/1 tsp five-spice powder	
10 ml/2 tsp chopped or grated fresh ginger root	
salt and freshly ground black pepper	
2 egg whites, lightly beaten	
50 g/2 oz/¹/₂ cup cornflour	
oil for frying	
30 ml/2 tbsp groundnut oil	
2 chilli peppers, chopped	
2 cloves garlic, chopped	
1 red pepper, diced	
1 green pepper, diced	
1 jar Chinese mixed pickles	
250 ml/8 fl oz/1 cup stock	

1 Cut the carp fillets into strips and marinate for 1 hour in the lemon juice, soy sauce, five-spice powder, ginger, salt and pepper. Drain.
2 Coat the fish with the egg whites and cornflour. Stir-fry in hot oil until cooked. Transfer to a serving dish.
3 Heat the groundnut oil and fry the chilli peppers, garlic, and peppers for 4 minutes. Add the mixed pickles and stock and bring to the boil.
4 Pour the hot sauce over the fish.

Photograph (top)

Squid with Vegetables

Serves 4
Preparation time: 45 mins
540 kcal

600 g/1¼ lb squid
1 bunch spring onions
100 g/4 oz celery
100 g/4 oz bamboo shoots
100 g/4 oz Chinese cabbage
100 g/4 oz beansprouts
30 ml/2 tbsp groundnut oil
100 g/4 oz bacon, diced
5 ml/1 tsp chopped or grated ginger root
1 chilli pepper, chopped
10 ml/2 tsp hoisin sauce
10 ml/2 tsp oyster sauce
250 ml/8 fl oz/1 cup stock
salt and freshly ground black pepper
a dash rice wine or sherry
10 ml/2 tsp cornflour
30 ml/2 tbsp water

1 Cut the squid into fine rings and the vegetables into bite-sized pieces.
2 Heat the oil, add the bacon and fry until crisp. Add the ginger and chilli peppers and stir-fry for 2 to 3 minutes.
3 Add the vegetables, beansprouts, bamboo shoots and squid rings.
4 Mix in the seasoning sauces and stock and bring to the boil. Season with salt, pepper and rice wine or sherry. Mix the cornflour and water, stir in and reheat gently until thickened.

Photograph (bottom)

Fried Fish in Hoisin Sauce

Serves 4
Preparation time: 45 mins
plus marinating
450 kcal

---

1 kg/2 lb sole or plaice fillets
45 ml/3 tbsp wine vinegar
salt and freshly ground black pepper
2 egg whites
10 ml/2 tsp cornflour
20 ml/4 tsp water
30 ml/2 tbsp baking powder
30 ml/2 tbsp groundnut oil
2 cloves garlic, chopped
1 bunch spring onions, chopped
45 ml/3 tbsp soy sauce
15 ml/1 tbsp hoisin sauce
5 ml/1 tsp chopped or grated ginger root

1 Cut the fish fillet into bite-sized pieces. Coat with wine vinegar, season with salt and pepper and leave for 15 minutes.
2 Mix the egg whites, cornflour mixed with water and a little baking powder. Pour over the fish and toss until coated.
3 Heat the oil and fry the fish a portion at a time. Remove to a plate.
4 Add the garlic and spring onions to the pan and stir-fry for 2 minutes.
5 Add the soy sauce, hoisin sauce and ginger then return the fish to the pan. Mix round gently and reheat briefly.

Photograph opposite (top)

Stir-Fried Scampi

Serves 4
Preparation time: 35 mins
465 kcal

---

450 g/1 lb scampi, shelled
30 ml/2 tbsp groundnut oil
400 g/14 oz Chinese cabbage or Savoy cabbage
2 cloves garlic, chopped
1 onion
2 carrots
5 ml/1 tsp chopped or grated ginger root
150 ml/¼ pt/⅔ cup rice wine or sherry
250 ml/8 fl oz/1 cup vegetable stock
30 ml/2 tbsp soy sauce
15 ml/1 tbsp oyster sauce
5 ml/1 tsp five-spice powder
10 ml/2 tsp cornflour
20 ml/4 tsp water
½ bunch parsley, chopped

1 Wash the scampi. Heat the oil and stir-fry the scampi for 2 minutes. Transfer to a plate.
2 Cut the onion, carrots and cabbage into strips.
3 Add to the pan with the garlic and stir-fry for 5 minutes.
4 Add the ginger, rice wine, stock, soy sauce, oyster sauce and five-spice powder then bring to the boil.
5 Stir in the cornflour smoothly mixed with water. Add the scampi and bring up to the boil, stirring. Sprinkle with parsley and serve.

Photograph opposite (bottom left)

Prawn with Tofu

Serves 4
Preparation time: 1 hour
530 kcal

4-6 wood ear mushrooms
1 onion
1 red pepper
1 green pepper
400 g/14 oz peeled prawns
juice of 1 lemon
30 ml/2 tbsp groundnut oil
200 g/7 oz minced pork
5 ml/1 tsp chopped or grated ginger root
salt and freshly ground black pepper
200 g/7 oz tofu, cubed
45 ml/3 tbsp soy sauce
45 ml/3 tbsp rice wine or sherry
10 ml/2 tsp oyster sauce
10 ml/2 tsp hoisin sauce
250 ml/8 fl oz/1 cup stock
10 ml/2 tsp cornflour
20 ml/4 tsp water

1 Soak the mushrooms in hot water for 45 minutes. Drain.
2 Cut the mushrooms and vegetables into strips. Sprinkle the prawns with lemon juice.
3 Heat the oil and stir-fry the pork and ginger for 5 minutes. Add the vegetables. Season with salt and pepper.
4 Mix in the prawns, tofu, seasoning sauces, rice wine or sherry and stock. Bring to the boil.
5 Blend the cornflour water, add to the pan and bring to the boil, stirring until thickened.

Photograph opposite (bottom right)

Crab Balls with Vegetable Noodles

Serves 4
Preparation time: 45 mins
plus standing
1130 kcal

225 g/*8 oz* Chinese ribbon noodles	
salt	
4 spring onions	
2 carrots	
100 g/*4 oz* celery	
100 g/*4 oz* mangetout	
450 g/*1 lb* crab	
200 g/*7 oz* streaky belly pork	
2 eggs	
60 ml/*4 tbsp* soy sauce	
15 ml/*1 tbsp* Oyster sauce	
150 ml/*¹/₄ pt/²/₃ cup* rice wine or sherry	
freshly ground black pepper	
2.5 ml/*¹/₂ tsp* five-spice powder	
a pinch of sugar	
30 ml/*2 tbsp* cornflour	
oil for deep-drying	
150 ml/*¹/₄ pt/²/₃ cup* groundnut oil	
30 ml/*2 tbsp* peanut butter	
20 ml/*4 tsp* hoisin sauce	
20 ml/*4 tsp* tabasco sauce or chilli sauce	

1 Soak the noodles for 10 minutes in hot water, then drain. Cook for 4 to 5 minutes in boiling salted water. Remove and drain well, spread out onto a baking sheet and leave to dry for 45 minutes in a cool oven or other warm place.

2 Clean the spring onions, carrots, celery and mangetout and cut them into chunks.
3 Mince the crab with the belly pork and transfer to a bowl.
4 Add the eggs, half the soy sauce, the oyster sauce and a dash of the rice wine or sherry and knead all the ingredients together thoroughly.
5 Season with a little more rice wine or sherry, pepper, five-spice powder and sugar. Add the cornflour and work thoroughly into the mixture.
6 With damp hands, shape the mixture into smallish balls and deep-fry in hot oil until cooked through and well browned. Remove from the pan, drain and keep warm.
7 Heat the groundnut oil in a pan, add the vegetables and stir-fry until light gold. Remove from the pan and keep warm.
8 Deep-fry the noodles until just soft then drain. Put into a clean pan, add the fried vegetables then stir in the peanut butter, remaining soy sauce, hoisin sauce, tabasco or chilli sauce and the remaining rice wine or sherry.
9 Season well with salt and pepper and arrange on a serving dish.
10 Top with the crab balls and serve immediately.

Scallops with Chicken Strips

Serves 4
Preparation time: 1 hour
380 kcal

4-6 dried Chinese mushrooms

2 chicken breast fillets

salt and freshly ground black pepper

5 ml/1 tsp five-spice powder

400 g/14 oz scallops

juice of 1 lemon

1 onion

1 small courgette

1/2 cucumber

4 tomatoes

30 ml/2 tbsp groundnut oil

30 ml/2 tbsp soy sauce

15 ml/1 tbsp oyster sauce

250 ml/8 fl oz/1 cup stock

10 ml/2 tsp cornflour

20 ml/4 tsp water

---

1 Soak the mushrooms in hot water for 45 minutes. Drain.
2 Cut the mushrooms and chicken into strips and season with salt, pepper and five-spice powder. Sprinkle the scallops with the lemon juice. Chop the vegetables.
3 Heat a little of the oil and stir-fry the chicken for 2 minutes. Add the scallops and stir-fry for 2 minutes. Remove from the pan. Add a little more oil and stir-fry the courgette, cucumber and tomatoes separately for 2 minutes.
4 Return everything to the pan and heat for 3 minutes.

5 Stir in the soy sauce, oyster sauce and stock. Mix the cornflour with the water, stir into the sauce and bring to the boil, stirring until thickened.

Photograph opposite (centre)

Fish with Bacon

Serves 4
Preparation time: 45 mins
830 kcal

---

1 x 1.5 kg/3 lb haddock

juice of 2 lemons

salt and freshly ground black pepper

30 ml/2 tbsp wine vinegar

2 onions, chopped

50 g/2 oz parsley, finely chopped

200 g/7 oz bacon, diced

1 bunch spring onions, chopped

100 g/4 oz cashew nuts

---

1 Sprinkle the fish with lemon juice and season.
2 Bring the wine vinegar and 1.5 l/2 1/2 pts /6 1/4 cups of water to the boil, add the onions and simmer for 5 minutes.
3 Mix in the parsley, add the fish and simmer gently for about 20 minutes.
4 Stir-fry the bacon, add the spring onions and cashew nuts and stir-fry for 1 minute.
5 Arrange the fish on a serving plate and top with the hot mixture.

Photograph opposite (top)

Red Mullet in White Sauce

Serves 4
Preparation time: 1 hour
460 kcal

6-8 dried Chinese mushrooms

1 red mullet

150 ml/1/4 pt/2/3 cup dry white wine

juice of 1 lemon

30 ml/2 tbsp wine vinegar

1 onion

2 carrots

200 g/4 oz celery

1 l/1 3/4 pt/2 1/2 cups stock

150 ml/1/4 pt/2/3 cup milk

10 ml/5 tsp cornflour

salt and freshly ground black pepper

---

1 Soak the mushrooms in hot water for 45 minutes. Drain and cut into strips.
2 Sprinkle the fish with wine, lemon juice and wine vinegar.
3 Cut the vegetables into chunks. Heat the stock, add the vegetables and bring to the boil.
4 Add the fish and simmer gently for 18 to 20 minutes. Drain.
5 Reserve 300 ml/1/2 pt/1 1/4 cups of stock and mix with half the milk. Pour into a clean pan. Mix the cornflour with rest of milk and add. Bring to the boil, stirring. Season with salt and pepper.
6 Spoon over the fish with the strained vegetables.

Photograph opposite (bottom)

Dim Sum

The Chinese kitchen is rich in little delicacies – dim sum – which are included in a menu or eaten in between courses. Here is a selection of some of the most delicious.

Vegetable Soup with Pork, page 56

Vegetable Soup with Pork

Serves 4
Preparation time: 40 mins
240 kcal

6-8 dried Chinese mushrooms

4 spring onions

2 carrots

50 g/2 oz celery

100 g/4 oz soy beansprouts

100 g/4 oz bamboo shoots

200 g/7 oz lean pork

1 l/1³/₄ pt/2¹/₂ cups stock

100 g/4 oz peeled prawns

salt and freshly ground black pepper

a pinch of ground ginger

5 ml/1 tsp five-spice powder

2 eggs, beaten

1 Soak the mushrooms in hot water for 45 minutes. Drain and cut into strips.
2 Cut the vegetables and pork into strips.
3 Heat the stock and add all remaining ingredients except prawns and simmer for 20 minutes.
4 Season and thicken by adding the eggs. Stir in the prawns, heat through and serve.

Photograph page 54

Spicy-Sour Soup

Serves 4
Preparation time: 1 hour
350 kcal

6-8 dried Chinese mushrooms

2 chicken breast fillets

20 ml/4 tsp groundnut oil

1 garlic clove, chopped

1 chilli pepper, chopped

1 onion, cut into strips

2 carrots, cut into strips

200 g/7 oz bamboo shoots, cut into strips

200 g/7 oz beansprouts

15 ml/1 tbsp tomato purée

1 l/1¹/₄ pts/4¹/₄ cups stock

30 ml/2 tbsp wine vinegar

5 ml/1 tbsp grated ginger root

30 ml/2 tbsp soy sauce

salt and freshly ground black pepper

a pinch of Cayenne pepper

100 g/4 oz transparent noodles, soaked

15 ml/1 tbsp cornflour

30 ml/2 tbsp water

1 Soak the mushrooms in hot water for 45 minutes. Drain and slice.
2 Cut the chicken fillets into strips.
3 Heat the oil and stir-fry the chicken for 3 minutes.
4 Add the garlic, chilli pepper, onion, carrots, bamboo shoots and beansprouts and stir-fry for 5 minutes.
5 Add the tomato purée, stock, wine vinegar, ginger and soy sauce and season. Stir-fry for 3 minutes.
6 Add the mushrooms.
7 Mix together the cornflour and water and stir it into the pan. Bring to the boil, simmer for 3 minutes.

Photograph opposite (top)

Steamed Stuffed Dumplings

Serves 4 to 6
Preparation time: 1¹/₂ hours
995 kcal

900 g/just under 2 lb unsweetened yeast dough, shop bought or home made

20 ml/4 tsp sesame oil

450 g/1 lb cooked minced pork

2 cloves garlic, chopped

5 ml/1 tsp chopped or grated ginger root

30 ml/2 tbsp soy sauce

30 ml/2 tbsp rice wine or sherry

15 ml/1 tbsp cornflour

salt and freshly ground black pepper

a pinch of Cayenne pepper

a pinch of sugar

1 Leave the dough to rise in a warm place until doubled in size.
2 To make the filling, heat the sesame oil and stir-fry the minced pork with the garlic and ginger.
3 Add the soy sauce, rice wine or sherry, cornflour, spices and sugar and stir-fry for 3 minutes.
4 Shape the dough into little rounds, put the filling in the centre and close up by pinching the edges well together. Shape into dumplings.
5 Steam in a bamboo basket for 15 to 20 minutes.

Photograph opposite (bottom)

Chicken Won-Tons

Serves 4
Preparation time: 20 mins
160 kcal

2 chicken breast fillets

4-6 dried Chinese mushrooms

4 spring onions

30 ml/2 tbsp Chinese picked vegetables

20 ml/4 tsp soy sauce

30 ml/4 tsp hoisin sauce

2.5 ml/¹/₂ tsp five-spice powder

15 ml/1 tbsp cornflour

salt and freshly ground black pepper

1 quantity Won-Ton dough or 1 packet filo pastry

1 Soak the mushrooms in hot water for 45 minutes. Drain.
2 Mince the chicken very finely with the mushrooms, spring onions and pickled vegetables. Transfer to a bowl.
3 Add the soy sauce, hoisin sauce and five-spice powder and season the meat mixture well with salt and pepper.
4 Stir in the cornflour and leave aside while you prepare the dough.
5 Roll out the dough and cut the dough or pastry into 4 cm/1¹/₂ in squares. Place a little filling on each, moisten the edges with water then bring the edges to the centre over the filling, completely enclosing it.

6 Poach in boiling salted water for 15 to 20 minutes or steam in a bamboo steamer. Alternatively, deep-fry in hot oil. Serve hot.

Photograph opposite (left)

Won-Ton Dough

Serves 4
Preparation time: 30 mins plus resting
250 kcal

225 g/8 oz/2 cups plain flour

1 egg

150 ml/¹/₄ pt/²/₃ cup water

a pinch of salt

1 Sieve the flour on to a work surface and make a hollow in the centre. Add the egg, water and a little salt and mix and knead everything into a pliable dough.
2 Wrap the dough in a damp tea towel and leave for at least 30 minutes in the refrigerator.
3 Remove the dough, roll out thinly and cut into 4 cm/1¹/₂ in squares.
4 When making the won-tons, place the filling on the dough squares, fold the corners to the centre. Close the won-tons and cook in salted water or deep-fry in hot oil.

> **Gourmet Tip**
> If you prefer, you can use filo pastry for the won-tons.

Prawn Won-Tons

Serves 4
Preparation time: 30 mins
310 kcal

100 g/4 oz dried Chinese mushrooms

30 ml/2 tbsp groundnut oil

100 g/4 oz minced pork

200 g/7 oz peeled prawns, chopped

1 onion, chopped

15 ml/1 tbsp tomato purée

5 ml/1 tsp soy sauce

5 ml/1 tsp five-spice powder

5 ml/1 tsp chopped or grated ginger root

20 ml/4 tsp cornflour

salt and freshly ground black pepper

1 quantity Won-Ton dough or 1 packet filo pastry

1 Soak the mushrooms in hot water for 45 minutes. Drain and chop.
2 Heat the oil and stir-fry the pork and prawns together for about 5 minutes.
3 Add the onion and mushrooms and dry for 3 to 4 minutes.
4 Add the tomato purée, soy sauce, five-spice powder and ginger and mix well. Bind with the cornflour, season to taste with salt and pepper and mix well.
5 Make and cook the prawn won-tons in the same way as the chicken won-tons.

Photograph opposite (right)

59

Crispy Spring Rolls

Serves 4
Preparation time: 1 hour
810 kcal

4-6 dried Chinese mushrooms

2 chicken breast fillets, finely chopped

4-6 spring onions, chopped

1 red pepper, diced

100 g/4 oz soy beansprouts

100 g/4 oz bamboo shoots, diced

30 ml/2 tbsp groundnut oil

30 ml/2 tbsp soy sauce

30 ml/2 tbsp hoisin sauce

5 ml/1 tsp five-spice powder

a pinch of Cayenne pepper

salt and freshly ground black pepper

a bunch of coriander, chopped

8 freshly-made pancakes

1 egg yolk, beaten

oil for deep-frying

1 Soak the mushrooms in hot water for 45 minutes. Drain and chop.
2 Heat the oil and stir-fry the chicken for 5 minutes. Add the vegetables and stir-fry for a further 4 minutes.
3 Stir in the soy sauce, hoisin sauce and season well with five-spice powder, Cayenne pepper, salt and pepper.
4 Mix in the coriander. Remove the filling from the heat and leave to cool.
5 Spread the filling equally on top of the pancakes and fold together in the following way: fold in the sides from the right and left, brush the edges with beaten egg yolk and roll up the pancakes.
6 Fry the pancake rolls in deep fat or in a frying pan until cooked. Serve immediately.

Fortune Cookies

Makes 12
Preparation time: 1 hour
140 kcal

*225 g/**9 oz**/2 cups plain flour*

*2.5 ml/**¹/₂ tsp** ground aniseed*

a large pinch of cardamom

a large pinch of ground cloves

a large pinch of salt

*75 g/**3 oz**/¹/₃ cup brown sugar*

3 eggs

*15 ml/**1 tbsp** groundnut oil*

lucky charms or slips of paper containing proverbs

oil for deep frying

1 Sieve the flour on to a work surface and sprinkle with aniseed, cardamom, cloves and salt.
2 Toss in the brown sugar then make a hollow in the centre. Put the eggs and the oil into the hollow.
3 Knead the ingredients together with floured hands to form a smooth dough.
4 Roll the dough out thinly on a floured work surface and cut into squares. Moisten the edges with water. Place a lucky charm or slip of paper on each then bring corners to the centre and press well together.
5 Heat the oil in a saucepan and fry the fortune cookies for a few minutes until golden. Remove from the fat and drain thoroughly.

GOURMET COOKSHELF...

...Pretty little books that make excellent "thank you" gifts. Or better still for your own Life Style uplift.

GOURMET COOKSHELF...

...For the kind of cook who seriously enjoys eating good food, but doesn't enjoy spending days in the kitchen to prepare.

GOURMET COOKSHELF...

...Books for cooks to collect, that will produce that uplifting recipe whenever you feel like something enticing.

◆ Regional Chinese Specialities

◆ Wok Specialities

◆ Cooking for One or Two

◆ Regional Italian Specialities

◆ Grills and Barbeques

◆ Spaghetti, Tagliatelle Etc...

◆ Fondues

◆ Pasta

◆ Desserts

◆ Finger Food

◆ Fish

◆ Sauces

and yet more to come — be sure of that!

For details write to:
W. Foulsham, Yeovil Road, Slough, Berkshire SL1 4JH.

Index of Recipes

foulsham
Yeovil Road, Slough, Berkshire, SL1 4JH

ISBN 0-572-01765-0

This English language edition copyright © 1992 W. Foulsham & Co. Ltd
Originally published by Falken-Verlag, GmbH, Niedernhausen TS, Germany
Photographs copyright © Falken-Verlag

Printed in Portugal